what do

Springs

do?

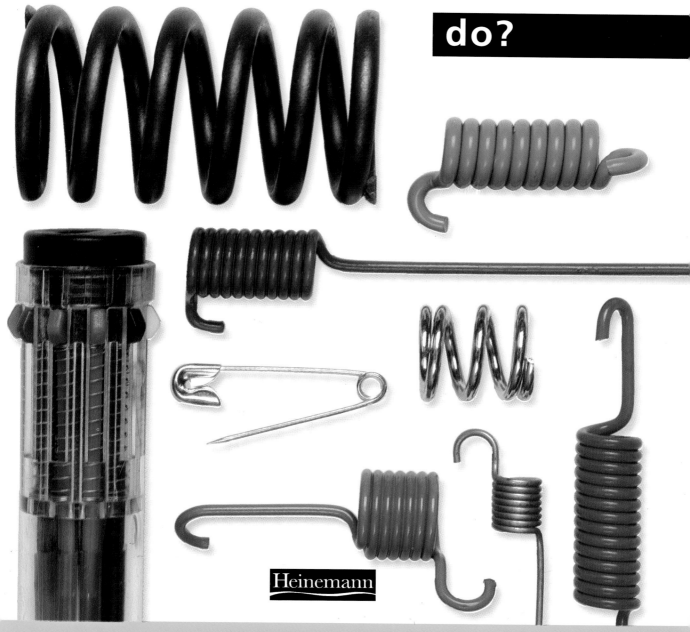

Heinemann

David Glover

First published in Great Britain by Heinemann Library
Halley Court, Jordan Hill, Oxford OX2 8EJ
a division of Reed Educational & Professional Publishing Ltd.

MELBOURNE AUCKLAND
FLORENCE PRAGUE MADRID ATHENS
SINGAPORE TOKYO SÃO PAULO
CHICAGO PORTSMOUTH NH MEXICO
IBADAN GABORONE JOHANNESBURG
KAMPALA NAIROBI

Designed by Celia Floyd and Sharon Rudd
Illustrated by Barry Atkinson (pp9, 11, 19) and Tony Kenyon (pp7, 15, 23)
Printed in the UK by Jarrold Book Printing Ltd., Thetford.

00 99 98 97 96
10 9 8 7 6 5 4 3 2 1

ISBN 0 431 06264 1

British Library Cataloguing in Publication Data
Glover, David
    What do springs do?
    1. Springs (Mechanism) – Juvenile literature
    I. Title II. Levers
    621.8 ' 24

Acknowledgements
The Publishers would like to thank the following for permission to reproduce photographs:
Trevor Clifford pp4, 5, 6, 9, 12, 14, 15, 17, 20, 21, 22, 23; Sealy p8; Colorsport p10; Spectrum Colour Library p16; Stockfile/Steven Behr p18; Zefa p19.
Cover photograph by Trevor Clifford.
Commissioned photography arranged by Hilary Fletcher.
Special thanks to Jack and Rose who appear in the photographs.

Thanks to David Byrne for his comments on the initial draft.

The Publishers would like to thank Do It All Ltd and Salisburys for the kind loan of equipment and material used in this book.

Every effort has been made to contact copyright holders of any material reproduced in this book. Any omissions will be rectified in subsequent printings if notice is given to the Publisher.

Contents

What are springs?

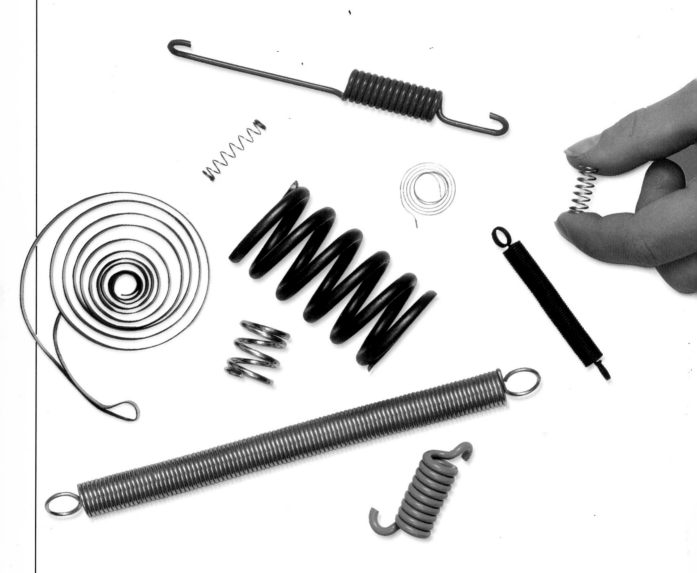

Most springs are made from metal wire or strips. If you squash a spring, stretch it, bend it or wind it up, it always tries to spring back into shape.

This jack-in-a-box is a spring toy. When you push it down into the box and fasten the lid, you are squashing its spring.

When you unfasten the catch, the spring makes the jack jump from its box. It can make you jump with surprise!

Pogo stick

A pogo stick has a strong spring that bounces you up in the air. A rubber foot stops the stick from slipping on the ground.

The spring on a pogo stick is a strong **spiral** of steel wire. Your weight squashes it down to make it shorter. The spring pushes back up as it tries to return to its normal shape. This force lifts you up into the air.

When you jump with a pogo stick, you squash the spring.

The spring pushes back up and bounces you into the air.

When you land, the spring squashes again ready for the next bounce.

Spring beds and chairs

Have you ever bounced on your bed? Many bed mattresses are filled with wire springs. These help you to sleep comfortably at night. When you lie on the bed, the springs squash to support every part of your body.

The springs on this chair make the seat soft and comfy. When you sit on this chair the springs stretch to hold up your weight.

Spring words

When a spring is made shorter, or squashed, we say that it is *compressed*. When a spring is made longer, or stretched, we say that it is in *tension*.

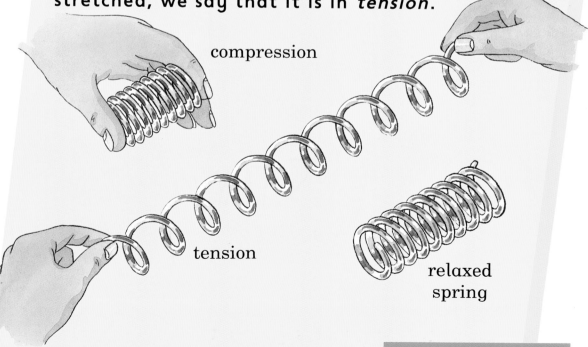

compression

tension

relaxed spring

Springboards

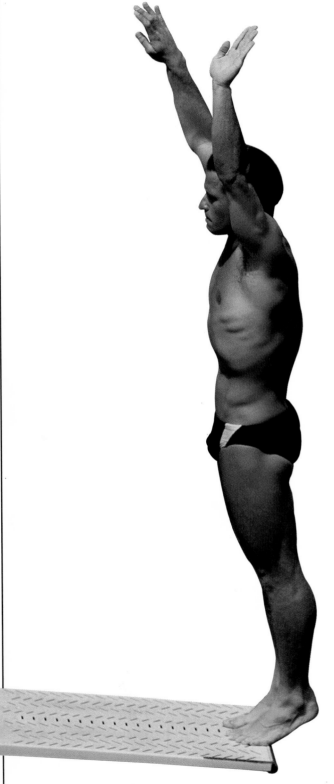

Springboards are springy, but they don't have springs.

This diver bounces on the springboard at the pool. As the diver bounces, the board bends and then springs back to push him into the air.

There is a wheel on the side of the board which moves forwards or backwards when turned round. This makes the springy part of the board either shorter or longer to give different amounts of bounce.

This springboard is made from springy wood. The gymnast jumps on it firmly to help her spring high over the bar.

FACT

A heavy person bends a springboard more than a light person. But when the board springs back they would each go the same height. It takes more spring to lift a heavy person.

FILE

Door springs and locks

This gate has a spring at the top. It pulls the gate shut when someone leaves it open.

This door has a spring at the bottom. It stops the door from banging against the wall when someone pushes it open too hard.

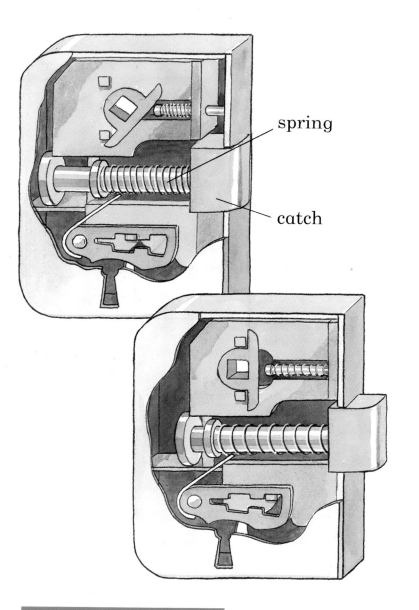

spring

catch

The door handle has a spring inside. When you turn the handle it pulls back the **catch**. When you let go of the handle the spring pushes the catch back into place.

The door spring and the catch spring work together to keep the door shut.

Spring loaded

This pen has a spring inside it. We say that the pen is **spring loaded**. When you press the button at the bottom, the pen tip comes out of the case. A spring tries to push the tip back inside, but a **catch** holds it in place. When you press the button again, this releases the catch and the tip goes back inside the pen case.

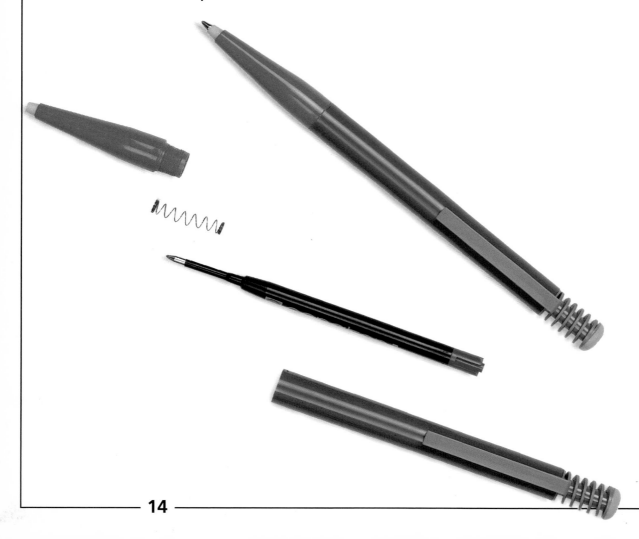

Spring-loaded umbrellas are handy for carrying in a small bag. When it rains, you take off the cover, release the catch and the umbrella springs open. A squashed spring inside the handle does all the work for you.

Springy hats!

In the nineteenth century some men wore spring-loaded top hats. When they went to the theatre they used to squash their tall hats and put them under the seats. When the play was over they let the hats spring back into shape.

Spring balances

A spring balance is a simple weighing machine that uses a spring. **Anglers** often use spring balances to weigh their fish.

The weight of the fish stretches the spring. The stretched spring turns a needle around a **dial**. The heavier the fish, the more the spring stretches and the further the needle turns.

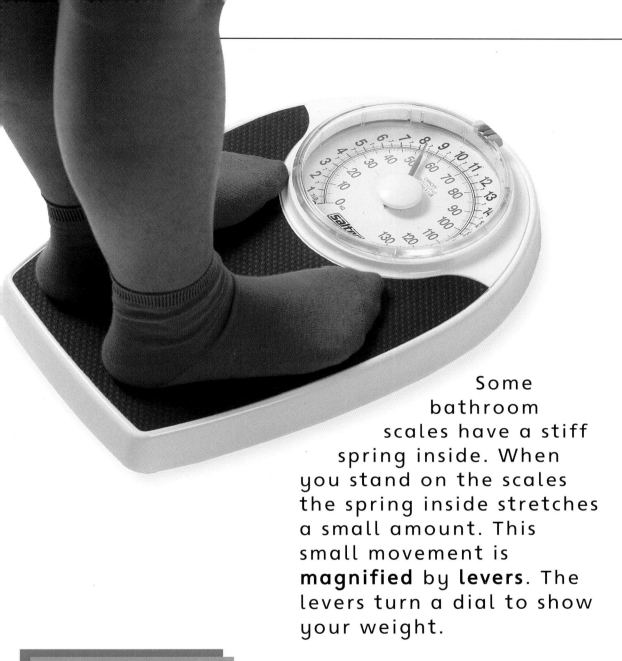

Some bathroom scales have a stiff spring inside. When you stand on the scales the spring inside stretches a small amount. This small movement is **magnified** by **levers**. The levers turn a dial to show your weight.

FACT

The spring on a spring balance gets longer when you add more weight. A two kilogram fish stretches the spring twice as much as a one kilogram fish.

FILE

Spring wheels

Some mountain bikes have springs in their **forks**. The springs squash and stretch when the wheels go over bumps and holes. This makes the ride more comfortable and lets you go faster.

Moto-cross bikes speed round a very rough course. They leap high in the air over the hills and hit the ground again with a jolt. Their long springs help to soften the landing for the rider.

Leaf springs

Special sets of springs were invented for horse-drawn carts. They helped to make the passengers comfortable. The springs were made from thin strips of metal stacked together like the leaves of a book.

Clockwork springs

You have to wind up
some old clocks with a
key. The key winds up a
spiral spring inside the
clock. As the wound-up
spring slowly unwinds, it
turns the clock hands.

spiral spring   key

The inside of a clock.

Clockwork toys use clock springs to make them move. The clock spring turns a **motor**. In the past, many wonderful toys were powered by clockwork motors. Now most moving toys have electric motors that are powered by **batteries**.

A wind-up radio!

Someone has just invented a clockwork radio that doesn't need batteries. A clockwork motor turns a tiny machine called a *dynamo*. The dynamo makes electricity. You can wind up the radio when you want to listen.

Pinballs and cannonballs

A spring fires the steel balls in a pinball machine. When you pull back the plunger it squashes the spring. When you let go, the plunger springs forward and pushes the ball up the table.

Human cannon balls are popular acts at the circus. Although it looks as if the clown is fired from a gun by **gunpowder**, this is only the flash of a firework. It is really a big spring inside the cannon that pushes the clown up into the air.

FACT

A staple gun has a strong spring inside. When you squeeze the handle you squash the spring. Then a catch releases the spring and the gun fires a staple to stick your poster to the wall.

FILE

Glossary

angler Someone who uses a rod and line to catch fish.

batteries Small packages of chemicals that make electricity.

catch The piece of metal that clicks into a slot to keep a door closed.

compressed When something is squeezed or squashed.

dial The part of a weighing machine where a pointer moves along a row of numbers to show you the weight.

dynamo A machine which makes electricity.

forks The pair of rods or arms that hold the front wheel of a bicycle.

gunpowder Powdered chemicals that burn with a flash and a bang.

lever A rod or a bar which turns around a hinge or pivot.

magnify To make bigger.

moto-cross bike A motor cycle for racing over rough ground.

motor A machine that uses electricity or fuels such as petrol or coal to make things move.

spiral A special shape that goes along and around at the same time. A corkscrew is a spiral shape.

spring loaded Held in place by a spring.

tension When something is being pulled or stretched.

work The energy you use to move something or wind something up.

Index